RUGBY

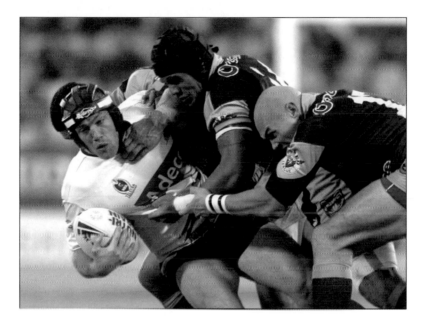

Frances Purslow

WEIGL PUBLISHERS INC.

Published by Weigl Publishers Inc.

350 5th Avenue, Suite 3304, PMB 6G

New York, NY 10118-0069

Library of Congress Cataloging-in-Publication Data

Purslow, Frances.

　For the love of rugby / Frances Purslow.

　p. cm. — (For the love of sports)

　Includes index.

　ISBN 1-59036-380-9 (hard cover : alk. paper) —

　ISBN 1-59036-381-7 (soft cover : alk. paper) 3656 /3 /3 10/07

1.　Rugby football—Juvenile literature.　I. Title. II. Series.

GV945.25.P87 2007　　796.333—dc22　　2005026968

Printed in the United States of America

1 2 3 4 5 6 7 8 9 10 09 08 07 06

Cover: Richard Haughton of the Saracens is tackled by Mark van Gisbergen of the Wasps during the Guinness Premiership Match on September 3, 2005, in London, England.

Editor

Frances Purslow

Cover and page design

Terry Paulhus

Contents

All about Rugby

Rugby is one of the most popular team sports in the world. It is played in more than 100 countries. Males and females of all ages play rugby for fun. Some also play for money. Running, passing, kicking, and tackling are all part of this fast-paced sport. Speed, strength, and stamina are important for rugby players to succeed. Many people think that all rugby players are big. This is not true. Some positions are filled by smaller players who run fast. Rugby is a sport for all sizes.

There is a legend that explains how rugby first began. It took place in the town of Rugby, England, in 1823. William Webb Ellis, a student at Rugby School, became frustrated during a soccer game. He grabbed the ball with his hands. This is against the rules in soccer. He carried the ball to the opponents' goal with the other team running close behind. A new sport was born.

Rugby first became popular among schoolboys in the 1830s and 1840s.

Rugby is a physical sport. It involves jumping, running, falling, and tackling.

For many years, people continued to play rugby. However, it was not an organized sport until 1871. That year, the Rugby Football Union was formed in England.

Soon there was a disagreement that led to two types of rugby being played. They are Rugby Union and Rugby League. Each type of rugby, or code, has its own set of laws, or rules. They also differ in the number of players on a team. Rugby Union is played in more countries than Rugby League, including the United States and Canada.

The Rugby Union is made up of roughly 2,000 clubs. They play more than 200,000 matches each year.

CHECK IT OUT

Read more about the history of rugby at
www.highschoolrugby.com
Click on Quick Guide to Rugby.

5

Getting Started

Rugby players wear uniforms when they play. They also wear some equipment under their uniforms. Rugby is a rough game, so it is called a **contact sport**. When a player has the ball, the other team tries to take it away. The ball is slightly rounder and larger than a football.

Some rugby players wear fingerless gloves in wet weather to help them grip the ball.

Players wear shorts and long socks that match the colors of their team.

Players wear rugby boots with studs in the bottom. The studs help grip the ground so the players do not slip on the grass.

A rugby ball is oval and made of four panels. The Rugby Union ball is slightly larger than the League's ball. It is 11 to 12 inches (28 to 30 centimeters) long and 23 to 24 inches (58 to 62 cm) around the middle.

Players wear a mouthguard to protect their teeth and help prevent a **concussion**.

Some locks, props, flankers, and eightmen wear scrum caps to protect their ears. Some wrap tape around their heads to hold their ears flat instead.

Rugby players wear jerseys with their number on the back. The number tells the player's position. Jerseys are made of tough material so they do not rip easily. Some players also wear light shoulder padding under their jerseys.

The Pitch

Rugby is played on a grass field called a pitch. It is a bit longer and wider than a football field. The pitches for both Rugby Union and Rugby League are 109 yards (100 meters) long, with a **try** zone at either end. However, the Union field is 1 yard (1 m) wider than the League field. White lines mark the outer boundary of the pitch.

Rugby League

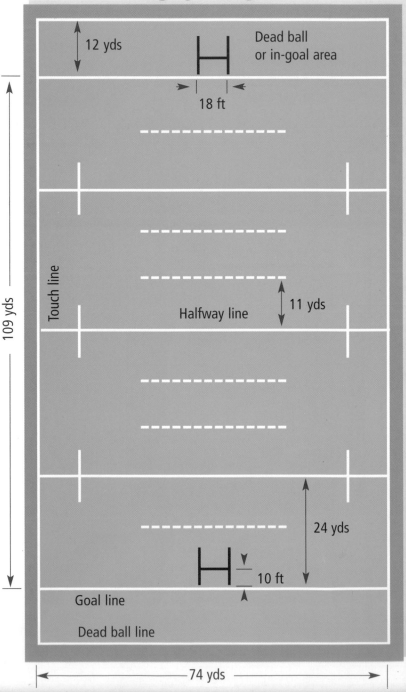

12 yds

Dead ball or in-goal area

18 ft

Touch line

109 yds

Halfway line

11 yds

24 yds

10 ft

Goal line

Dead ball line

74 yds

Rugby Union

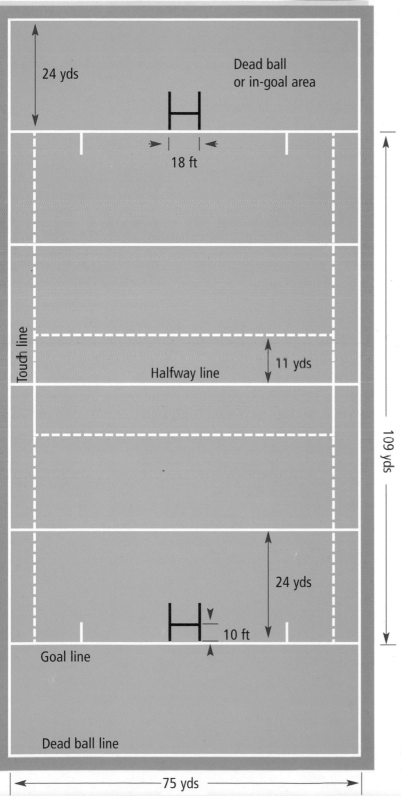

24 yds

Dead ball
or in-goal area

18 ft

Touch line

Halfway line

11 yds

109 yds

24 yds

10 ft

Goal line

Dead ball line

75 yds

Goalposts are set on the goal line at either end of the pitch. The goalposts are shaped like the letter "H." The posts are 18 feet (5.6 m) apart. There is a crossbar connecting them 10 feet (3 m) above the ground. The goalposts are usually covered with padding, so players will not be hurt if they run into them.

The Rugby Union's try zone is twice as long as the Rugby League's.

Rugby Basics

A rugby game is called a match. One referee oversees the match. It is played in two 40-minute halves with a 5-minute halftime. After halftime, the teams switch ends. The team with the most points wins the match.

There are many laws in the sport of rugby, but the main goal is to score tries. This happens when the ball carrier runs across the goal line and touches the ball on the ground. A try is also scored if the ball bounces into the try zone and a player for the other team reaches it first and presses it to the ground. A try is worth five points in Rugby Union, four in Rugby League.

To signal that a try has been scored, the referee raises his arm while blowing the whistle.

Point Chart		
	Rugby Union	Rugby League
Try	5 points	4 points
Conversion	2 points	2 points
Drop goal	3 points	1 point
Penalty kick	3 points	2 points
Penalty try	5 points	4 points

Officials wait in the try zone when the ball is kicked. They raise their flags when a kick scores points.

In Rugby Union, the lineout is used to get the ball back in play after it goes out of bounds. One of the tallest players on each team, usually a lock, is lifted to catch the ball thrown in from the sidelines.

After a try is scored, the **kicker** kicks the ball to gain more points for his or her team. Kickers can **place kick** or **drop kick** the ball as far out from the goal line as they want, but it must line up with where the ball was touched down in the try zone. If the ball goes through the goalposts, the team gains two points.

Another way to gain points is with a **penalty kick**. The final way for a team to score points is a drop goal. At any time, any player can try to drop kick the ball through the uprights. This means that for any of these kicks to be successful, they must pass between the posts and above the crossbar.

If play is stopped due to an **infraction**, the **forwards** take part in a scrum to get the ball back in play. They get into formation and bend over at the waist. At a signal from the referee, they engage or interlock with the forwards of the other team. Each group tries to overpower the other with its strength. The ball is rolled into the opening between the feet of the two groups. Then each team tries to hook it to a teammate outside of the scrum. The ball is then passed to one of the backs.

A rugby ball cannot be passed forward. Players can carry it forward or kick it forward, but they can only pass it to teammates beside or behind them.

Positions on the Pitch

In Rugby Union, each team is made up of eight big forwards and seven smaller, faster backs, for a total of 15 players. In Rugby League, there are only six forwards plus seven backs. Special skills make players good at certain positions.

There are no flankers in Rugby League.

The numbers on players' jerseys tell the position each one plays. The forwards wear numbers 1 to 8. The two props are numbers 1 and 3. They are big, strong players at the front of the scrum. They also lift players in lineouts. Between the props is the hooker. This front rower hooks the ball with his or her foot during the scrum and directs it to the scrum half. The second row consists of two locks. These are the tallest players. They jump for the ball during lineouts. On either side of the locks are numbers 6 and 7. These flankers are powerful and have good ball-handling skills. The eightman is at the back of the scrum. He or she directs and controls the scrum.

The forwards of each team take part in the scrum. They use their strong leg muscles for power.

The backs wear numbers 9 to 15. They use their strong leg muscles to reach top speed quickly and avoid being tackled by the other team. The scrum half is similar to a quarterback in football. He or she rolls the ball into the scrum and watches for the hooker to pass it back out. The scrum half then must decide in a split-second which teammate is in the best position to receive the ball. The fly half is one of the speedy backs who run, pass, and kick the ball. Wings are numbers 11 and 14. They are fast runners and must be good kickers. The two centers are **agile** and can change direction without warning. They are also good ball handlers and tacklers. Number 15 is the fullback. He or she is a strong kicker and **aggressive** runner.

Championships

Many boys and girls play rugby on community teams. When they are older, they play on high school teams and may move on to college or university teams. They can also play at the club level. The coaches of these teams help develop rugby stars of the future. In North America, leagues have games and tournaments that are **endorsed** by USA Rugby or Rugby Canada.

Many cities in North America have **Super League** teams. Scouts watch these teams to select players for the U.S. or Canadian national teams. When a player plays for his or her country in an international match, the player receives a cap.

The three key international rugby tournaments are the World Cup, Six Nations, and Tri-Nations.

A few players have received as many as 100 caps in their rugby careers.

The first World Cup was hosted by New Zealand and Australia in 1987. In the World Cup, teams measure themselves against the best players of other nations. Twenty teams from different countries compete for the Webb Ellis Cup, named for the boy who started the sport of rugby. The winning team is declared world champion. The event occurs every four years and is watched by more than 3 billion people around the world.

The Rugby Canada men's team took part in all five Rugby World Cups. The USA Eagles participated in four, missing out in 1995. The Women's Rugby World Cup also occurs every four years. However, it is held on different years than the men's.

The countries involved in the Six Nations Championship are England, Ireland, Scotland, Wales, France, and Italy. It was first played in 1880, which makes it the oldest rugby tournament in the world.

The Webb Ellis Cup is the biggest prize in rugby. This trophy is named after the legendary inventor of the sport.

The Tri-Nations Series was first played in 1996. Every year since then, Australia's Wallabies, New Zealand's All Blacks, and South Africa's Springboks host two games apiece, for a total of six games in all.

Before their matches, the New Zealand All Blacks perform a native dance called the Haka.

Superstars of the Sport

The sport of rugby has attracted many superb athletes. They thrill fans who fill the stands.

SERGE BLANCO

POSITION
Fullback
TEAM
Les Bleus of France

Career Facts:

- Serge was born in Caracas, Venezuela, on January 31, 1958.
- He played for Les Bleus of France between 1980 and 1991. He represented France in international tournaments 93 times during those years.
- Serge was called the superman of rugby. He scored 233 points for France during his career.
- He was inducted into the Rugby Hall of Fame in 1997.

GARETH EDWARDS

POSITION
Scrum-half
TEAM
Welsh National Team

Career Facts:

- Gareth played for the national team of Wales from 1967 to 1978.
- He received 53 caps over his career, 10 of which he earned playing for the British Lions from 1968 to 1974.
- Born in 1947, Gareth was inducted into the Rugby Hall of Fame 50 years later.

MICHAEL JONES

POSITION:
Flanker
TEAM
New Zealand
All Blacks

Career Facts:
- Born in Auckland, New Zealand, Michael played for Samoa against Wales in 1986.
- He played for the New Zealand All Blacks from 1987 to 1998.
- Michael played in many tournaments, including the 1991 World Cup.
- His nickname is "The Iceman."

DAN LYLE

POSITION
Eightman
TEAMS
USA Eagles; Bath and
Leicester in England

Career Facts:
- Dan switched from football to rugby when he was in his 20s.
- He played for the USA Eagles in 1994 against Ireland.
- Then Dan turned professional and played in England for Bath and Leicester.
- He retired after the 2003 World Cup.

CHECK IT OUT

Discover more about the USA Eagles at

www.usarugby.org

Superstars of Today

Rugby heroes of today have inspired young athletes to try this exciting sport.

MARTIN JOHNSON

POSITION
Lock
TEAM
British Lions

Career Facts:

- Martin is 6 feet 6 inches tall (1.98 m) and weighs 260 pounds (118 kilograms).
- He is the only player to captain two British Lions teams, in 1997 and 2001.
- Martin received 84 caps over his career playing for England between 1993 and 2003.
- Martin recently retired from rugby and was inducted into the Rugby Hall of Fame in 2005.

JOSH LEWSEY

POSITION
Wing/Fullback
TEAM
England

Career Facts:

- Josh is 5 feet 11 inches tall (1.8 m) and weighs 189 pounds (85.7 kg).
- Josh won his first cap at 21 years of age. He played for England in Australia in 1998.
- In 2003, he played in the World Cup and scored five tries. This tied England's try-scoring record.

JEN CRAWFORD

POSITION
Fullback/Center
TEAM
USA Eagles;
Berkeley All Blues

Career Facts:

- Jen was the captain of the USA Eagles when they played in the finals of the 1998 Women's World Cup.
- She was captain of the Berkeley All Blues when they competed in six consecutive USA Rugby National Women's Club Championships.
- Jen has earned 23 caps representing the United States in international tournaments.
- Since her retirement as a player in 2002, Jen has turned to coaching rugby.

ANDY FARRELL

POSITION
Center/Second Row
TEAMS
Wigan Warriors and the Saracens

Career Facts:

- For 14 years, Andy played for Wigan in the British Rugby League. Then, in March 2005, he switched to England's Rugby Union, and is now playing for the Saracens.
- In 2004, Andy was awarded the Golden Boot award as the world's top player.
- Andy hopes to play for England in the 2007 World Cup.
- He has won 34 Great Britain caps, 29 as captain. In 2004, he won the Rugby League's Man of Steel award for the second time.

CHECK IT OUT

To read more about some of these players, go to

www.rugbyhalloffame.com

Staying Healthy

There is a great deal of running in rugby, so players have to keep their bodies in good shape. They eat healthy foods and drink plenty of water. Eating balanced meals helps athletes work harder for longer periods of time.

The night before a match, many athletes eat **carbohydrates**, such as pasta, bread, and rice. The body stores this type of food as energy in the muscles and helps keep players from tiring during a match.

Fruits and vegetables provide vitamins and minerals to keep athletes healthy.

High-energy foods help athletes replace the energy they burn playing sports.

Foods from the other food groups, such as fruits and vegetables, protein, and milk products, also have important **nutrients** needed for a healthy body. Strong bones and muscles are important when playing a sport that requires speed and strength.

Athletes need to drink water to replace what they lose when they sweat. When muscles work hard, they produce heat in the body. To keep cool, the body releases heat through sweat.

Most teams begin a rugby match with drills to warm up specific parts of their bodies.

Rugby Brain Teasers

Test your rugby knowledge by trying to answer these brain teasers!

Q Which player rolls the ball into the scrum?

A The scrum half rolls the ball into the scrum.

Q Why do rugby players wear mouthguards?

A Players wear mouthguards to protect their teeth and help prevent concussions.

Q What is the name of the dance the New Zealand All Blacks perform before each match?

A The name of the dance is the Haka.

Q What are the two types of rugby codes?

A The two codes are Rugby Union and Rugby League.

Q What do rugby players call the field they play on?

A It is called the pitch.

Q How many points is a try worth?

A A try is worth five points in Rugby Union and four points in Rugby League.

Glossary

aggressive: likely to take chances

agile: able to move with quickness and ease

carbohydrates: foods that provide energy

concussion: an injury to the brain from being hit on the head

contact sport: a sport in which physical contact is allowed

drop kick: a kick in which the ball is dropped from the player's hands

endorsed: supported

forwards: players wearing numbers 1 through 8

infraction: an error or a broken rule

kicker: the fly half or fullback (number 10 or 15) who kicks the ball for a conversion

nutrients: substances needed by the body and obtained from food

penalty kick: a place kick that occurs after a penalty is called and the kicker thinks he is within range

place kick: a kick in which the ball is placed on a plastic tee on the ground

Super League: teams that represent their city

try: goal

Index